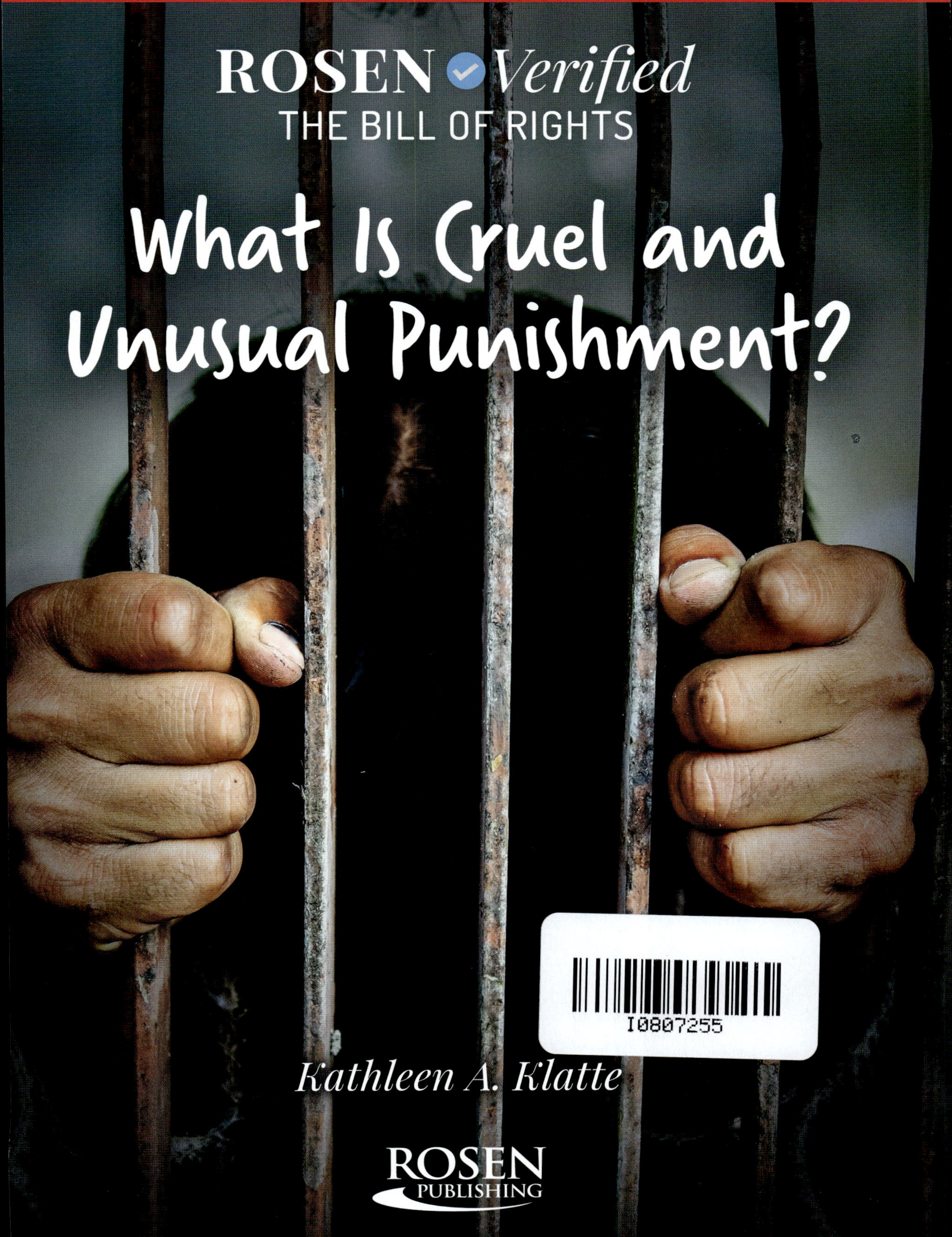

ROSEN Verified
THE BILL OF RIGHTS

What Is Cruel and Unusual Punishment?

Kathleen A. Klatte

ROSEN PUBLISHING

Published in 2024 by The Rosen Publishing Group, Inc.
2544 Clinton Street, Buffalo, NY 14224

First Edition

Editor: Greg Roza
Book Design: Michael Flynn

Photo Credits: Cover Chaikom/Shutterstock.com; (series background) PinkPueblo/Shutterstock.com; p. 5 https://commons.wikimedia.org/wiki/File:Drawing_of_William_de_Marisco.jpg; p. 7 Everett Collection/Shutterstock.com; p. 9 https://commons.wikimedia.org/wiki/File:TheSalemMartyr-Noble.jpg; p. 11 dba87/Shutterstock.com; p. 13 Chris Lawrence Travel/Shutterstock.com; p. 14-15 Artem Ermilov/Shutterstock.com; p. 16 https://commons.wikimedia.org/wiki/File:Anthony_Salerno.jpg; p. 17 zimmytws/Shutterstock.com; p. 19 https://commons.wikimedia.org/wiki/File:Marshalsea_prison,_London,_18th_century_(2).jpg; p. 21 https://commons.wikimedia.org/wiki/File:Monsieur_Madeleine_par_Gustave_Brion.jpg; p. 23 Lionel Deng/Shutterstock.com; p. 25 https://commons.wikimedia.org/wiki/File:Lyndon_Johnson_signing_Civil_Rights_Act,_July_2,_1964.jpg; p. 27 RuslanKphoto/Shutterstock.com; p. 29 https://commons.wikimedia.org/wiki/File:Oklahomacitybombing-DF-ST-98-01356.jpg; p. 31 Thx4Stock/Shutterstock.com; p. 32 Casimiro/Shutterstock.com; p. 33 https://commons.wikimedia.org/wiki/File:Tennessee_v._John_T._Scopes_Trial-_Outdoor_proceedings_on_July_20,_1925,_showing_William_Jennings_Bryan_and_Clarence_Darrow._(2_of_4_photos)_(2898243103).jpg; p. 35 RozenskiP/Shutterstock.com; p. 37 https://commons.wikimedia.org/wiki/File:Earl_Warren_Portrait,_half_figure,_seated,_facing_front,_as_Governor.jpg; p. 39 Zolnierek/Shutterstock.com; p. 41 sirtravelalot/Shutterstock.com; p. 43 Roman Motizov/Shutterstock.com; p. 45 zef art/Shutterstock.com.

Cataloging-in-Publication Data

Names: Klatte, Kathleen A.
Title: What is cruel and unusual punishment? / Kathleen A. Klatte.
Description: New York : Rosen Publishing, 2024. | Series: Rosen verified: the Bill of Rights | Includes glossary and index.
Identifiers: ISBN 9781499469783 (pbk.) | ISBN 9781499469790 (library bound) | ISBN 9781499469806 (ebook)
Subjects: LCSH: United States. Constitution. 8th Amendment--Juvenile literature. | Capital punishment--United States--Juvenile literature. | Punishment--United States--Juvenile literature.
Classification: LCC KF4558 8th K53 2024 | DDC 345.73'0773--dc23

Manufactured in the United States of America

Some of the images in this book illustrate individuals who are models. The depictions do not imply actual situations or events.

CPSIA Compliance Information: Batch #CSRYA24. For further information contact Rosen Publishing at 1-800-237-9932.

CONTENTS

The Eighth Amendment

The Eighth Amendment is another reminder that the Founding Fathers of the United States lived in a very different world than we do today. We have laws protecting, or safeguarding, people **suspected** of committing, or doing, crimes. People **convicted** of serious, or grave, crimes also have certain rights. Prisons are supposed to be clean, and inmates are supposed be fed and receive proper medical, or health, care. In states that permit the death penalty, **execution** should be quick.

THE TEXT OF THE EIGHTH AMENDMENT

Excessive bail shall not be required, nor excessive fines **imposed**, nor cruel and unusual **punishments** inflicted.

In the 18th century, prisons were often dangerous, dirty places. Diseases, or illnesses, were common. Execution methods were designed, or planned, to cause as much pain as possible. The movie *Braveheart* has a horrible scene of Scottish knight William Wallace's execution. He was hung, drawn, and quartered. That was the punishment for **treason** still in effect in England at the time of the American **Revolution** (1775–1783). The Founding Fathers wanted their new nation to be a better place.

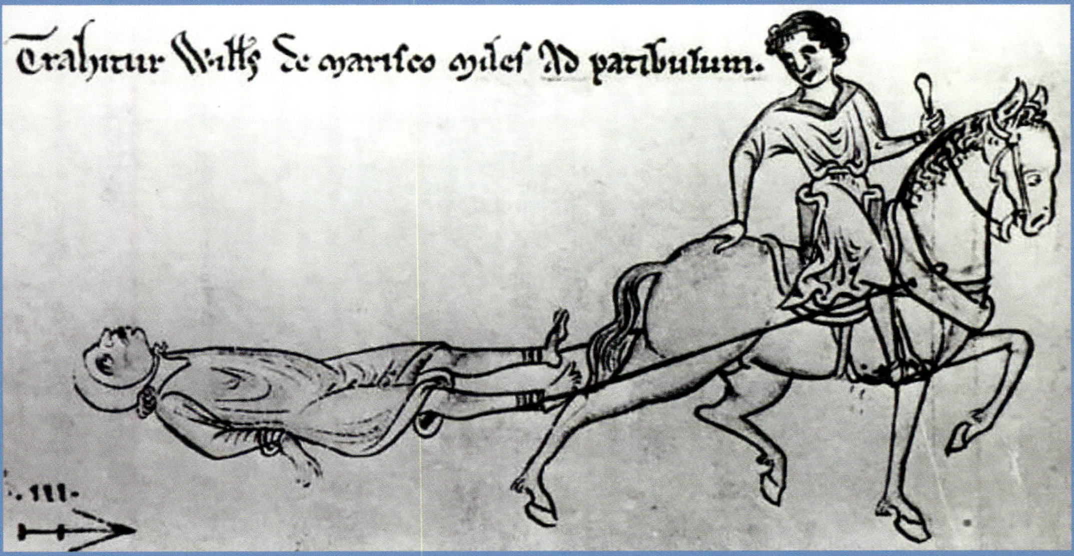

This illustration, or drawing, shows a person being "drawn" to his execution. "Quartering" meant the person was cut into four pieces.

The Bill of Rights

The first 10 amendments, or changes, to the Constitution are called the Bill of Rights. These are rights **guaranteed** to all Americans. People considered them so important that they needed to be listed in the Constitution. In fact, people in some states refused to **ratify** the Constitution unless the Bill of Rights was added.

The Bill of Rights was inspired by earlier documents, or pieces of writing, including:

The Magna Carta	England	1215
The English Bill of Rights	England	1689
The Virginia Declaration of Rights	Colony of Virginia	1776

GREAT CHANGE

The Founding Fathers lived in a time of great change. New inventions improved many businesses. Great writers and thinkers came up with new ways of looking at the world. The new nation could also grow. The Founding Fathers knew that laws would need to change over time. Article V of the Constitution allows for those changes.

James Madison (1751–1836) wrote the Bill of Rights. He was later the fourth president of the United States.

The World of the Founding Fathers

In the late 1700s, the world was a very different place. People convicted of serious crimes weren't always sent to prison. Instead, they were often given corporal punishment. This included things like flogging, or whipping. Flogging was a legal, or lawful, punishment in England until 1948.

Hanging was a common form of execution in the 18th century. Burning, as well as hanging, drawing, and quartering, were legal forms of capital punishment in England, although they were reserved for very serious crimes.

WHAT IS TRANSPORTATION?

In the 18th century, some criminals were **sentenced** to transportation. That meant they were deported, or forced to leave their country, to live in a colony. From the 17th century until the American Revolution, criminals (or anyone believed to have committed a crime) could be shipped off to the North American colonies.

From 1692 to 1693 in Salem, Massachusetts, over 200 people, mostly women, were accused of, or blamed for, being witches. Twenty people were executed. Their accusers burned some, drowned some, and crushed others with rocks.

Capital Punishment in the 18th Century

Capital punishment is the **judicial** practice of sentencing a convicted criminal to be executed. In our society, execution is saved for the worst crimes, such as murder. However, many states have outlawed the death penalty, or made it against the law. When a death sentence is issued, it can be **appealed**. Most modern executions are designed to be quick and somewhat painless.

Hanging was a common form of execution in the 18th century. The drop gallows, in which the prisoner stands on a trapdoor that opens and drops them suddenly, was introduced in 1760. Prior to that, hanging meant the prisoner choked to death because of their own body weight. It wasn't a quick or painless death.

DON'T LOSE YOUR HEAD

Before the invention of the guillotine, shown in this picture, convicted criminals might be beheaded with a sword or ax. Wealthy prisoners could pay for a swordsman to execute them quickly. An untrained axman might need several blows before the person died.

The guillotine was used for executions during the French Revolution (1789–1799). The idea behind it was that anyone sentenced to death would be executed quickly and painlessly.

The Enlightenment

Like many other educated people in the 18th century, the Founding Fathers were interested in the ideas of the Enlightenment. This was a movement of thinkers and scientists who tried to understand the world through **logic** and observation, or close study.

John Locke and other thinkers questioned ideas based on **superstition** and **tradition**. They thought all human beings had rights. They thought education was a key to improving people's lives. They weren't very popular with royalty or the church.

IN THE DECLARATION

The Declaration of Independence features many of John Locke's ideas. He believed that all people had certain rights. The idea that government holds power by the consent of the people is also one of his ideas.

John Locke (1632–1704) was an English philosopher, or thinker. He believed that democracy was a just form of government.

Bail Money

Bail is money a person who's charged with a crime must pay so they can leave jail until their trial, or court hearing. The U.S. legal system is supposed to be based on the idea that people are innocent until proven guilty. Bail is a way to make sure that someone accused of a crime returns to face their time in court.

Bail is set or denied, or refused, by a judge during a first hearing, which is called an arraignment. The amount of bail is decided partly by how bad the crime in question is. A person accused of a **violent** crime with strong evidence against them might be denied bail.

COURT TERMS

- **evidence** - Something that shows that something else is true.
- **guilty** - Having been found to have done something wrong in a court of law.
- **innocent** - Free from blame or fault.

A flight risk is someone a judge thinks might leave the **jurisdiction** before their trial. This can mean a person who could easily afford to travel. It might mean a person who owns their own boat or plane.

United States v. Salerno

United States v. Salerno was a 1987 Supreme Court ruling about the excessive (unfairly high) bail clause of the Eighth Amendment. Anthony Salerno was denied bail because he was part of a family that had already been very involved in crime. The judge felt that he was too dangerous to be allowed to go free in the community.

ANTHONY SALERNO

Salerno appealed the decision on the grounds that he was entitled, or deserved, to post bail and be released. However, the U.S. Supreme Court ruled that his rights under the Fifth and Eighth Amendments hadn't been violated, or broken.

FAST FACT

The 1984 Bail Reform Act says that a suspect doesn't have to be released on bail if the government can prove they're a danger to the community.

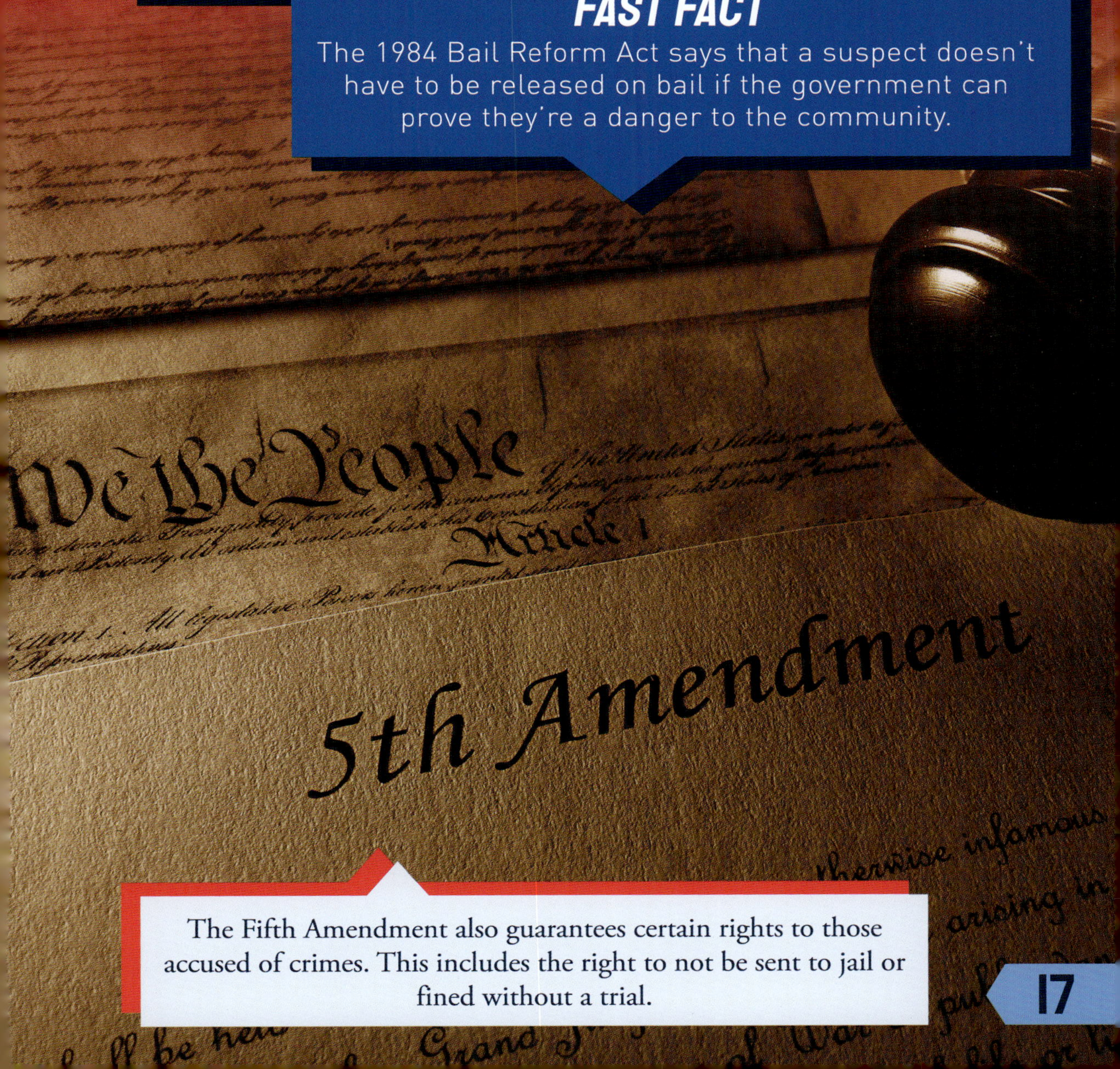

The Fifth Amendment also guarantees certain rights to those accused of crimes. This includes the right to not be sent to jail or fined without a trial.

The Excessive Fines Clause

The excessive fines clause of the Eighth Amendment refers to, or talks about, fines collected as punishment for breaking certain laws. The fine should fit the amount of harm or damage caused by the crime. It should be enough of a punishment to stop the person from committing the crime again.

In 1909, the Waters-Pierce Oil company appealed a fine of $1.6 million. The court ruled that the fine was relevant and not excessive. The company made money during the time the crimes in question were committed. The fine wasn't enough to force the company to close or cause undue hardship.

AN IMPORTANT CASE

United States v. Bajakajian is a 1998 Supreme Court ruling that overturned a fine. The court ruled that a fine of $357,144 was excessive under the Eighth Amendment. It exceeded the fine imposed, or placed on, someone else for a similar crime by hundreds of thousands of dollars. In addition, the crime in question was nonviolent.

Marshalsea Prison in London was open for 500 years. People who couldn't pay their debts, or bills, were imprisoned there. Often, they were held for many years for small debts.

Let the Punishment Fit the Crime

In the last century, the Eighth Amendment has been used to make sure that crimes are punished fairly.

Weems v. United States is a Supreme Court ruling from 1910. It set the idea that a punishment must be **proportional** to the crime that was committed. In this case, Paul Weems was sentenced to 15 years hard labor for a nonviolent crime. The court decided that the punishment was too harsh, or hard, for the crime of making fake documents.

Les Miserables is a novel, or story, by Victor Hugo. The main character, Jean Valjean, shown, was imprisoned for 19 years for stealing a loaf of bread. Do you think that's a fair punishment?

G. Brion 1862

Defining Cruel and Unusual

What exactly does "cruel and unusual punishment" mean? That's a question people have argued about for a long time. The Founding Fathers probably meant things like burning as a form of execution. They would also have been aware of prisons in Europe where people were imprisoned without trial.

At the time of the American Revolution, English law punished many offenses, or crimes, by hanging. There were no adjustments, or changes, under the law for children or disabled people.

SIGNED BY THE KING!

A lettre de cachet was an order from the king. Usually, it was an order to imprison someone. There was no trial and no legal way to appeal the king's decision. The use of lettres de cachet ended during the French Revolution.

VERIFIED

Amnesty International is a human rights organization. They work against the use of **torture** and the death penalty. You can find out more at **amnesty.org**.

The Bastille was a prison in Paris. In the 17th and 18th centuries, people could be imprisoned there with no trial or hope of parole. Parole is the early release of a prisoner who has behaved while in jail.

Evolving Standards of Decency

The words "evolving standards of decency" were used by Supreme Court Chief Justice Earl Warren in 1958. They mean that society changes over time. What was once acceptable doesn't always remain that way.

The Founding Fathers likely thought that execution by torture was cruel and unusual. That's something our society still agrees with today. However, they lived at a time when it was also legally and socially acceptable to enslave other human beings. That's no longer acceptable in our society. As peoples' views changed, laws changed.

Segregation is the separation of a race or group in schools and businesses. This was once legal in the United States. Segregation was legally ended by the Civil Rights Act of 1964.

SEAL OF THE PRESIDENT OF THE UNITED STATES

Changing Times

Over time, many court cases have changed what we view as acceptable punishment for crimes. Today, juvenile, or youthful, offenders can't be sentenced to death. If they're sentenced to life in prison, they must still have the chance for parole.

The Eighth Amendment also protects **intellectually** disabled people who may not be responsible for their actions or understand the **consequences**.

NOTABLE COURT CASES

***Graham v. Florida* - 2010**
It's unconstitutional to sentence a juvenile non-**homicide** offender to life without parole.

***Panetti v. Quarterman* - 2007**
A person can't be executed if they don't have a rational understanding of what's happening.

***Atkins v. Virginia* - 2002**
It's illegal to execute someone who's intellectually disabled.

***Coker v. Georgia* - 1977**
It's generally illegal to execute someone for **rape**.

The Eighth Amendment also covers prison conditions. How much force is needed to maintain order? Are prisons too crowded for inmates to receive proper medical care? These are questions that may be affected by the Eighth Amendment.

The Death Penalty

As of 2023, 27 states, the federal government, and the military allow the death penalty. At this time, the death penalty is saved for violent crimes, such as murder and **terrorism**. Many people think that execution is a fair punishment for such crimes.

The courts allow convicted criminals to appeal their sentences. This is intended as a safeguard against an innocent person being executed. However, appeals can take years. Some people think it's a form of cruel and unusual punishment for convicts to wait so long.

VERIFIED

World Day Against the Death Penalty is observed every October 10. It's organized by the World Coalition Against the Death Penalty. You can learn more about this group at **worldcoalition.org**.

Timothy McVeigh was sentenced to death for the 1995 bombing of the Alfred P. Murrah Federal Building in Oklahoma City. There were 168 deaths. Among them were 19 children in the building's daycare center.

Wilkerson v. Utah

Wilkerson v. Utah was an 1878 Supreme Court case. It considered what forms of execution were cruel and unusual. Wallace Wilkerson was found guilty of first-degree murder and sentenced to death by firing squad.

The court ruled that being shot to death didn't result in long suffering. Justices compared it to legal punishments at the time the Constitution was written. The Founding Fathers would have been aware of things like drawing and quartering. This is probably what they had in mind when considering the Eighth Amendment. In contrast, being shot to death is relatively quick.

The U.S. military can sentence people to the death penalty for serious crimes. The last military execution was in 1961. A U.S. Army private was hanged after being convicted of rape and attempted murder.

LEGAL FORMS OF EXECUTION

There are currently five forms of execution that are legal in the United States:

- lethal injection (use of deadly drugs)
- lethal (deadly) gas
- electrocution (use of electricity)
- firing squad
- hanging

The ACLU

The American Civil Liberties Union (ACLU) is a group that seeks to preserve, or maintain, Americans' constitutional rights. The ACLU was founded in 1920. It's been part of most major civil rights issues. The ACLU has been part of some of the most famous Supreme Court cases in American history.

ACLU lawyers have argued on behalf of the right to privacy and freedom of speech. Sometimes they represent unpopular groups. They do this to prove that everyone deserves fair representation under the law.

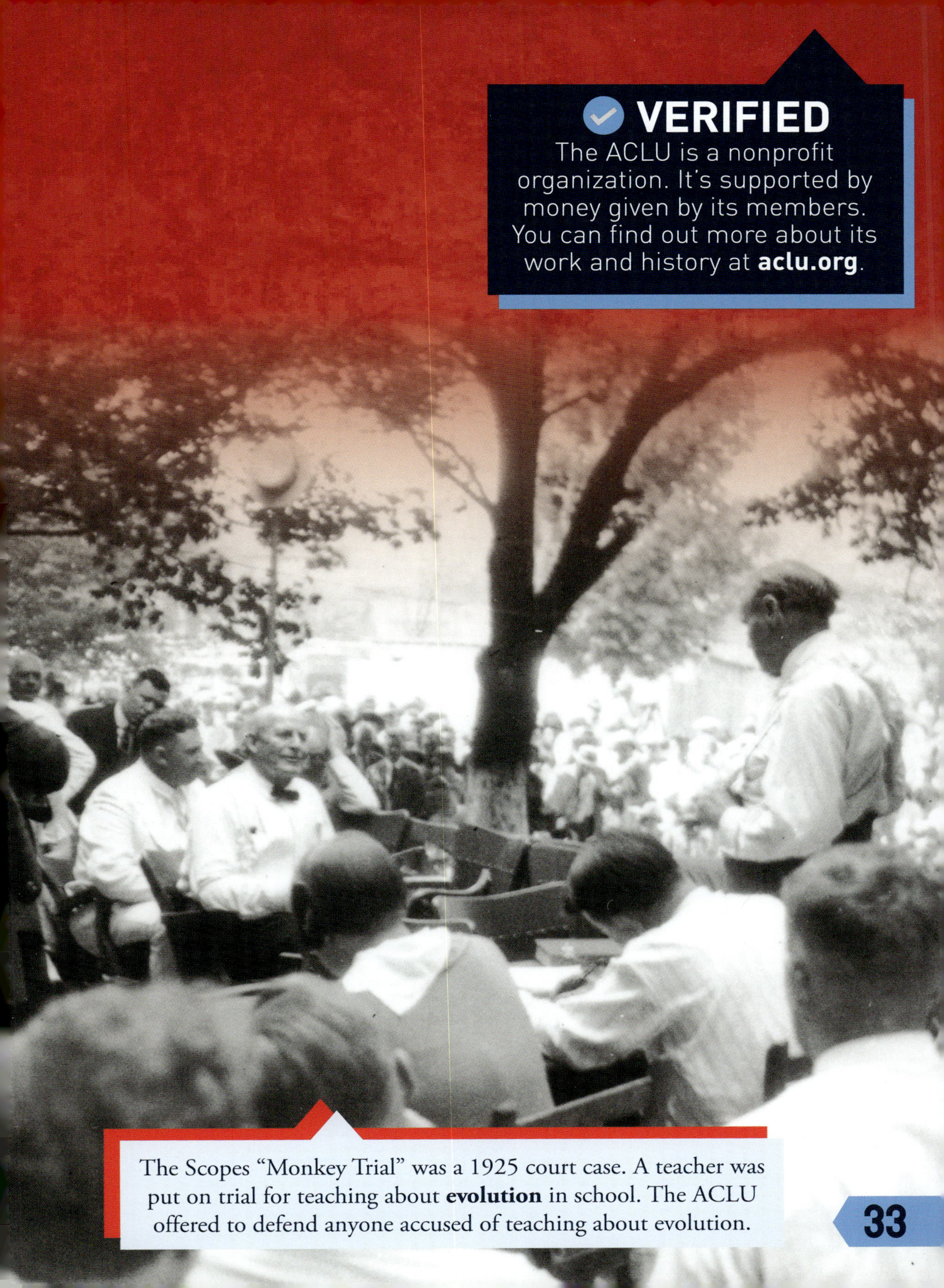

VERIFIED

The ACLU is a nonprofit organization. It's supported by money given by its members. You can find out more about its work and history at **aclu.org**.

The Scopes "Monkey Trial" was a 1925 court case. A teacher was put on trial for teaching about **evolution** in school. The ACLU offered to defend anyone accused of teaching about evolution.

The United States Supreme Court

The Supreme Court is the most important court in the United States. It generally doesn't hear cases about things like bank robberies or muggings. Sometimes it decides if a lower court has applied the law correctly in a case. The Supreme Court can reverse, or turn aside, another court's decision if it thinks the decision was unconstitutional.

The Supreme Court is currently made up of nine judges called justices. They're appointed, or selected, by the president. The Senate must approve the appointments. Supreme Court justices serve until they die or retire.

FAST FACT

The Supreme Court can overturn a law that's unconstitutional. This is called judicial review.

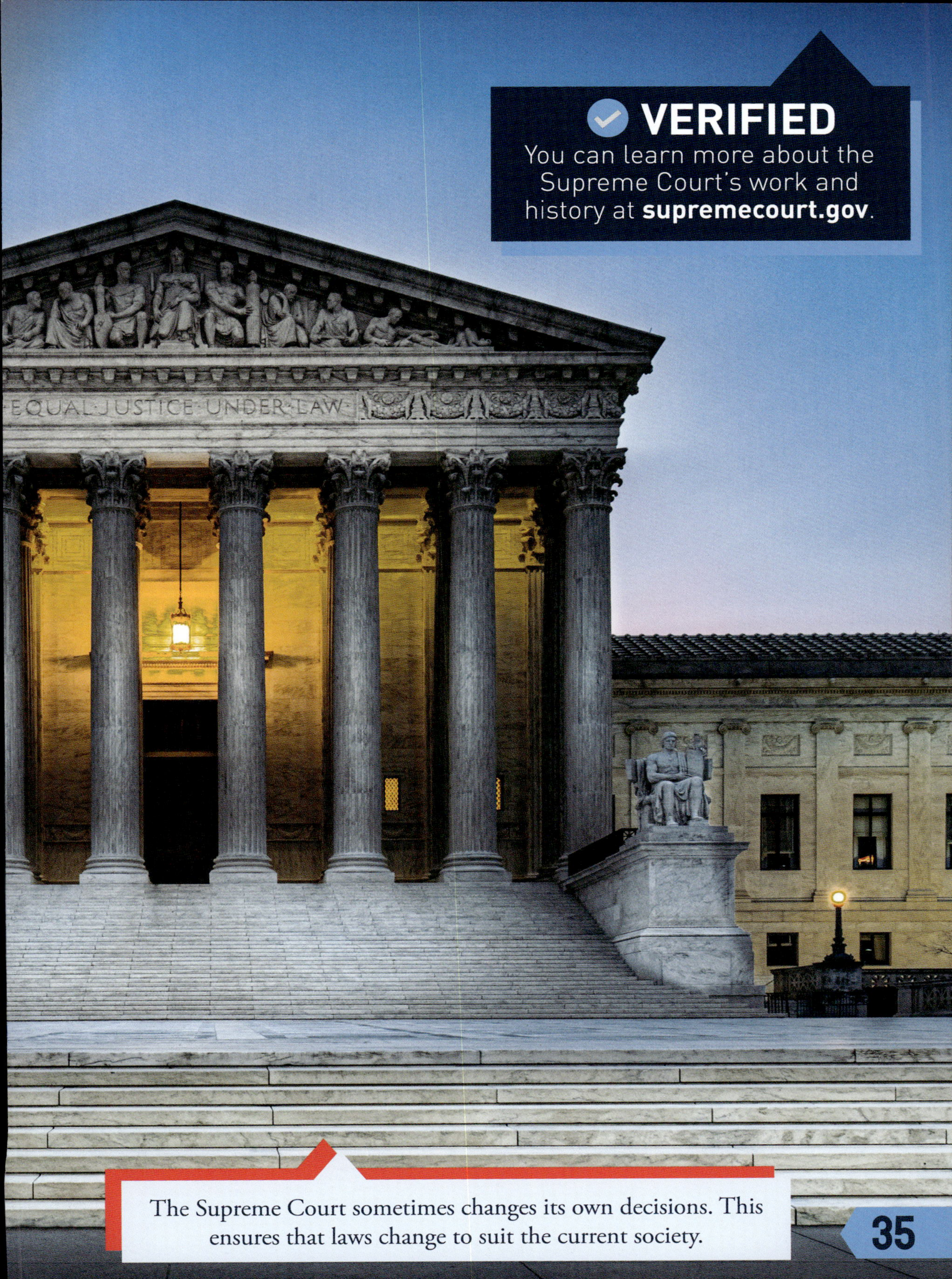

VERIFIED
You can learn more about the Supreme Court's work and history at **supremecourt.gov**.

The Supreme Court sometimes changes its own decisions. This ensures that laws change to suit the current society.

Trop v. Dulles

Trop v. Dulles was a 1958 court case. It concerned what was considered a cruel and unusual punishment. Alfred Trop deserted the U.S. Army. This is when someone leaves the military before their time is up. The Nationality Act of 1940 said that deserters lost their citizenship. When Trop was unable to get a **passport** on the grounds that he was no longer a U.S. citizen, he appealed the decision.

The Supreme Court ruled that taking away someone's citizenship was cruel and unusual. It said that this removed a person's place in society, effectively taking away all their rights.

Trop v. Dulles is the case in which Chief Justice Earl Warren (1891–1974) first wrote about "evolving standards of decency."

Due Process

The Fifth Amendment says that no one can be fined or imprisoned without "due process of the law." The Fourteenth Amendment says that due process applies to the states as well as the federal government. This means that U.S. laws and procedures apply to everyone. It also means that a state can't make a law that violates, or goes against, rights guaranteed in the Constitution.

Due process means that a person can't be arrested unless they've broken a law. They can't be sent to prison without a trial. People convicted of similar crimes should receive similar punishments.

DUE PROCESS AND THE EIGHTH

Because of the Fourteenth Amendment's due process clause, the Bill of Rights applies to state governments as well as the federal government. This means the Eighth Amendment applies to the states.

In 1972, the Supreme Court ruled that the death penalty was being used too freely for some groups of people. It also ruled that the death penalty is not necessarily cruel and unusual punishment. The Fourteenth Amendment allows each state government to make its own laws about the death penalty. As of 2023, the death penalty is legal in 27 states.

Justice is depicted, or shown, wearing a blindfold and holding scales. This shows that the law is supposed to apply equally to everyone.

True or False?

A police officer can arrest someone "just because."

False

A police officer can only arrest someone for breaking a law. They must tell the person what law they're accused of, or blamed for, breaking.

A person who's been arrested has rights.

True

A person accused of a crime has rights. One of the most important is the right to have a lawyer to help them.

A judge can order any punishment they like for a crime.

False

Punishments are supposed to be fair. They can't be violent or cruel by society's standards.

A judge's decision is final.

False

People can appeal a judgement they think is unfair. There are civil rights groups that can help with this process.

WHAT IS BURDEN OF PROOF?

People aren't supposed to need to prove their innocence in a trial. The government needs to prove them guilty. This is called the "burden of proof." A "burden" in this case means a responsibility, or something someone needs to take care of. "Proof" means a detail about the case has been proven to be a fact.

People convicted of crimes have rights. This is true. However, people convicted of serious crimes do lose some rights. Depending on their crime, some rights can be restored, or given back, after they serve their sentence.

Furman v. Georgia

Furman v. Georgia was a 1972 Supreme Court case about the death penalty. There were three men accused in the case. Two had been convicted of rape. One had been convicted of murder. All three had been sentenced to death. Their lawyers argued that the death penalty was applied in different ways for different crimes. They also argued that people of color and poor people were more likely to receive harsher sentences.

The court decided that there needed to be clearer laws about which crimes had the death penalty. There also needed to be a process to consider the record of the person being sentenced.

VERIFIED

The National Association for the Advancement of Colored People (NAACP) is a civil rights organization. It works within the court system to change laws that are unfair. Learn more at **naacp.org**.

The death penalty wasn't used again until 1976. *Gregg v. Georgia* was tried under new laws. Many standards had to be met before the judge issued the sentence.

Fair Treatment Under the Law

Everyone has the right to live in a safe community. But people who are accused or convicted of crimes have rights too. They must be treated fairly by the law.

You might wonder why we have laws like the Eighth Amendment to protect people accused of crimes. Think about this. What if you were accused of a crime? What if you were innocent? Or what if you made a mistake?

You'd want bail you could afford to pay. You'd want a trial. You'd want the judge to consider all the facts. You'd want to know that you could appeal an unjust decision. You'd want to know that the punishment for any crime you committed was fair.

Some recent Eighth Amendment cases have concerned whether execution by lethal injection is cruel and unusual. Many people feel that any form of execution is wrong. What do you think?

GLOSSARY

appeal: To bring a case to a higher court for review.

consequence: Something that happens because of a certain action or set of conditions.

convict: To find or prove that someone has committed a crime.

evolution: A natural process of change in plants and animals.

execution: The act of putting someone to death, especially as a legal punishment.

guarantee: A formal promise that certain conditions will be fulfilled.

homicide: A killing of one human being by another.

impose: To force somebody to accept a punishment or charge.

intellectual: Having to do with thought and the mind.

judicial: Having to do with a system of courts and laws.

jurisdiction: The limits or territory within which a person or group can exercise authority.

logic: A proper or reasonable way of thinking about or understanding something.

passport: A government-issued document that allows someone to travel to and return from foreign countries.

proportional: Being fitting in size, amount, or strength.

punishment: The pain or suffering someone is subjected to for having done wrong.

rape: The act of having sexual relations by force.

ratify: To formally approve.

revolution: The overthrow of one government that is replaced by a new government.

sentence: To impose a judgement on someone in a court. Also, the punishment imposed on that person.

superstition: A belief resulting from ignorance, fear of the unknown, or trust in magic.

suspect: To think someone might have done something or committed a crime.

terrorism: The use of fear and violence as a means of achieving a political goal.

torture: The causing of great pain especially to punish or get information from.

tradition: Having to do with the ways of doing things in a culture that are passed down from parents to children.

treason: The crime of attempting to overthrow the government of one's country.

violent: Using physical force in a way meant to cause harm to someone.

INDEX